EXPLORING COUNTRIES

CHINA

Tracy Vonder Brink

TABLE OF CONTENTS

A Crabtree Seedlings Book

Crabtree Publishing
crabtreebooks.com

School-to-Home Support for Caregivers and Teachers

This book helps children grow by letting them practice reading. Here are a few guiding questions to help the reader with building his or her comprehension skills. Possible answers appear here in red.

Before Reading:

- What do I think this book is about?
  - *I think this book is about China.*
  - *I think this book is about places to visit in China.*

- What do I want to learn about this topic?
  - *I want to learn where China is.*
  - *I want to learn about China's capital.*

During Reading:

- I wonder why...
  - *I wonder why emperors lived in the Forbidden City.*
  - *I wonder why the Great Wall is so long.*

- What have I learned so far?
  - *I have learned that China is in Asia.*
  - *I have learned that Shanghai is China's biggest city.*

After Reading:

- What details did I learn about this topic?
  - *I have learned that Beijing is more than 3,000 years old.*
  - *I have learned that giant pandas live in some mountains in China.*

- Read the book again and look for the vocabulary words.
  - *I see the word **temples** on page 6, and the word **bamboo** on page 18. The other glossary words are on pages 22 and 23.*

CHINA

China is a country.

It is in **Asia**.

BEIJING
CHINA

Beijing is the **capital**.

The city is more than 3,000 years old.

Most people in China speak Mandarin.

Beijing has many **temples**.

This building is part of the Temple of Heaven.

Emperors once ruled China.

They lived in a part of Beijing called the Forbidden City.

People visit it today.

Shanghai is China's biggest city. It is on the **coast**.

More than 24 million people live in Shanghai.

The Great Wall of China is in the North.

It is more than 13,000 miles (21,000 km) long.

China has many rivers.

The Yangtze River is the longest.

The land near the river is used to grow wheat, rice, and more.

China has many mountains.

The Himalayas are in the West.

The world's highest mountain is in the Himalayas.

Giant panda bears live in some mountains in China.

They eat **bamboo**.

Red pandas also live there. But they are not bears.

Red pandas belong to their own animal family.

China also has **deserts**.

The Gobi Desert is the largest desert in Asia.

China is a big country!

Glossary

Asia (AY-zhuh): The continent between Europe and Africa on one side and the Pacific Ocean on the other

bamboo (bam-BOO): A tall plant with hard, hollow stems

capital (KAP-i-tl): The city where the government of a country or a state is located

coast (kohst): The land next to the ocean or sea

desert (DEH-zert): A very dry area that gets a small amount of rain per year

emperors (EM-pr-urs): Rulers

temples (TEM-pls): Buildings in which people worship God or a god

Index

About the Author

Tracy Vonder Brink

Tracy Vonder Brink loves to visit new places. She has never visited China, but she enjoys Chinese food. She lives in Cincinnati, Ohio, with her husband, two daughters, and two rescue dogs.

Written by: Tracy Vonder Brink
Designed by: Rhea Magaro
Series Development: James Earley
Proofreader: Melissa Boyce
Educational Consultant: Marie Lemke M.Ed.

Photographs: All images from Shutterstock

Crabtree Publishing

crabtreebooks.com 800-387-7650

Printed in the U.S.A./062024/CG20240201

Published in Canada
Crabtree Publishing
616 Welland Avenue
St. Catharines, Ontario
L2M 5V6

Published in the United States
Crabtree Publishing
347 Fifth Avenue
Suite 1402-145
New York, New York, 10016

Library and Archives Canada Cataloguing in Publication
Available at Library and Archives Canada

Library of Congress Cataloging-in-Publication Data
Available at the Library of Congress

Hardcover: 978-1-0398-4479-7
Paperback: 978-1-0398-4560-2
Ebook (pdf): 978-1-0398-4632-6
Epub: 978-1-0398-4702-6
Read-Along: 978-1-0398-4772-9
Audio: 978-1-0398-4842-9